THIS BOOK BELONGS TO:

____

____

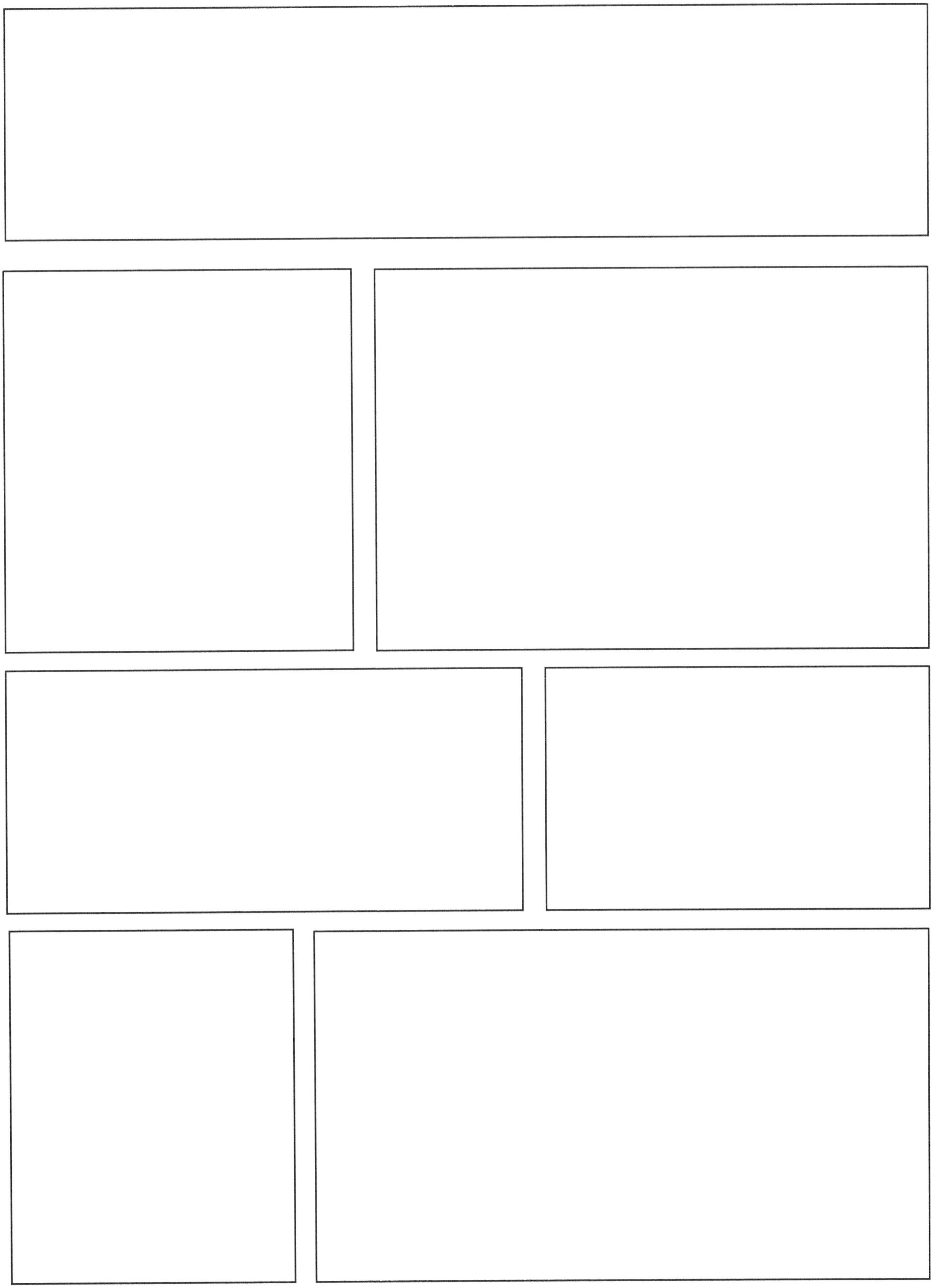

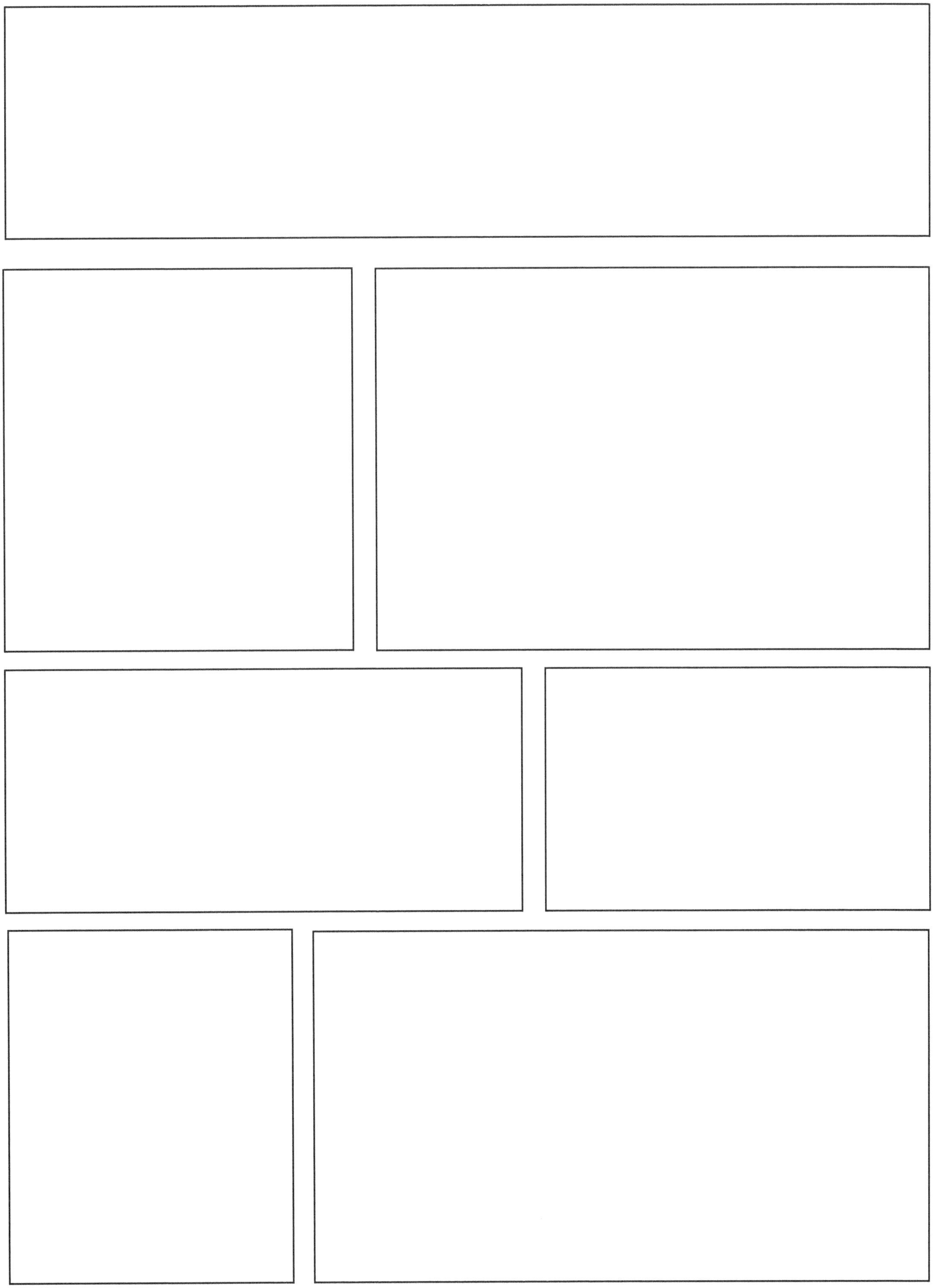

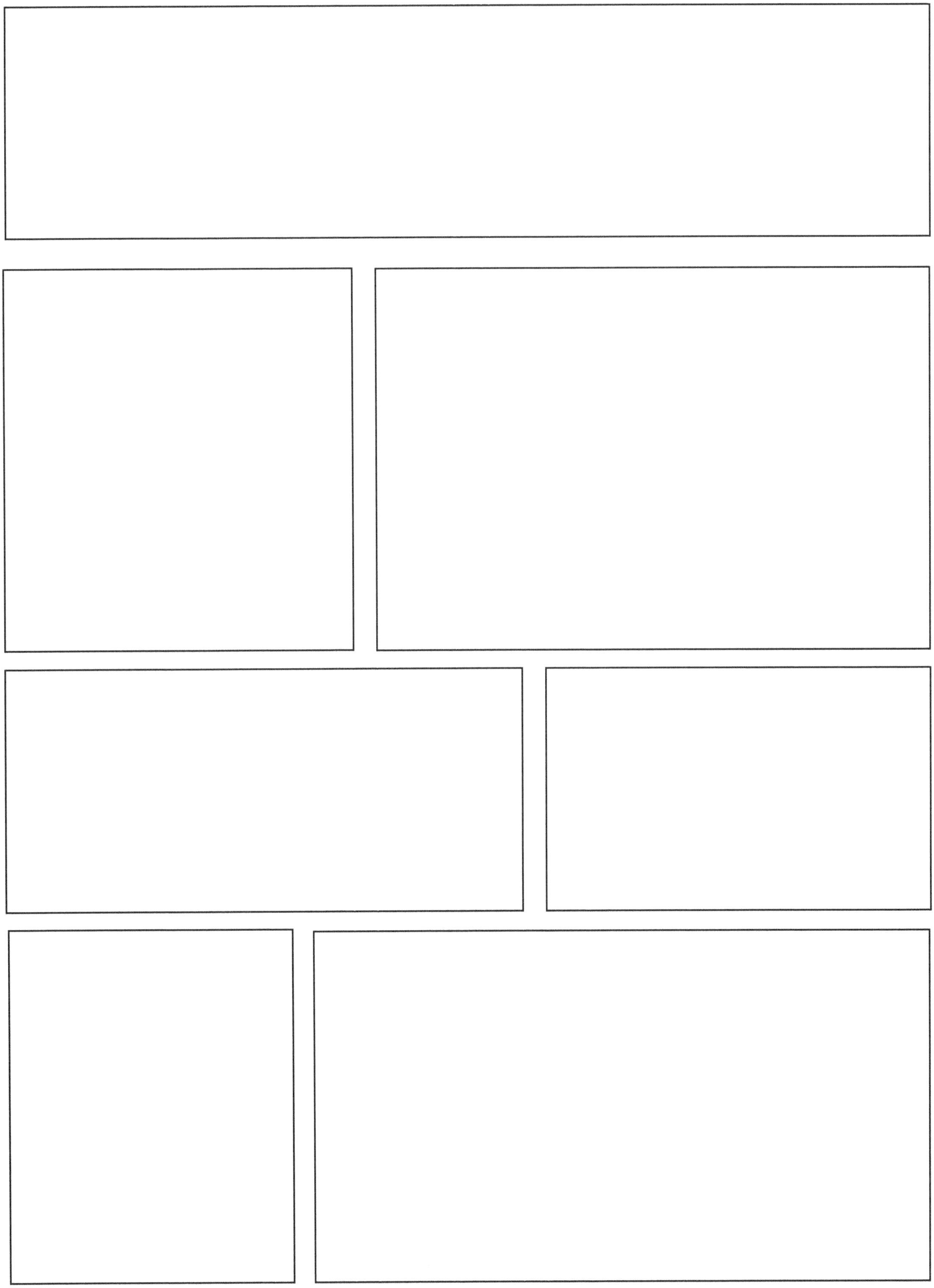

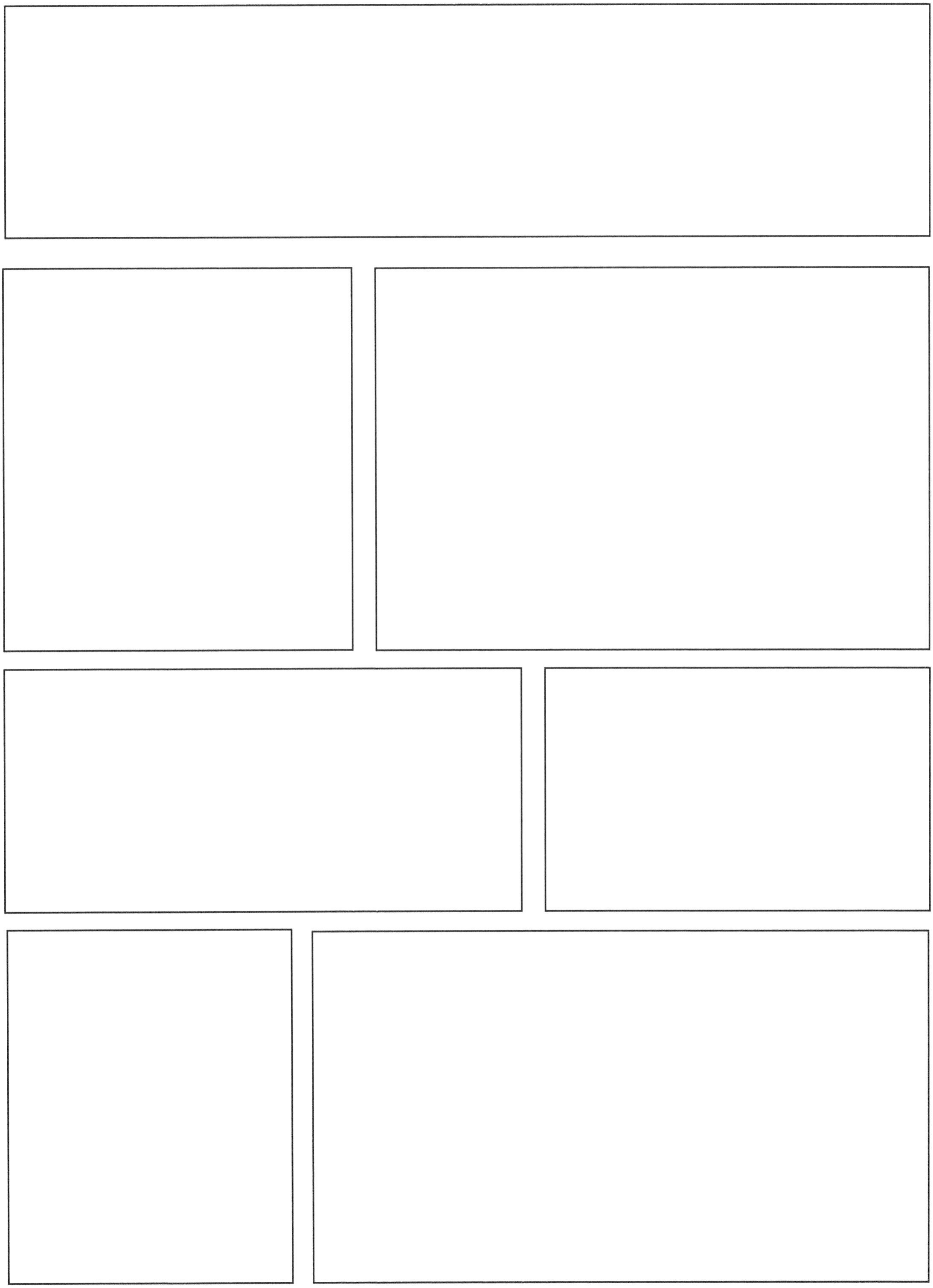

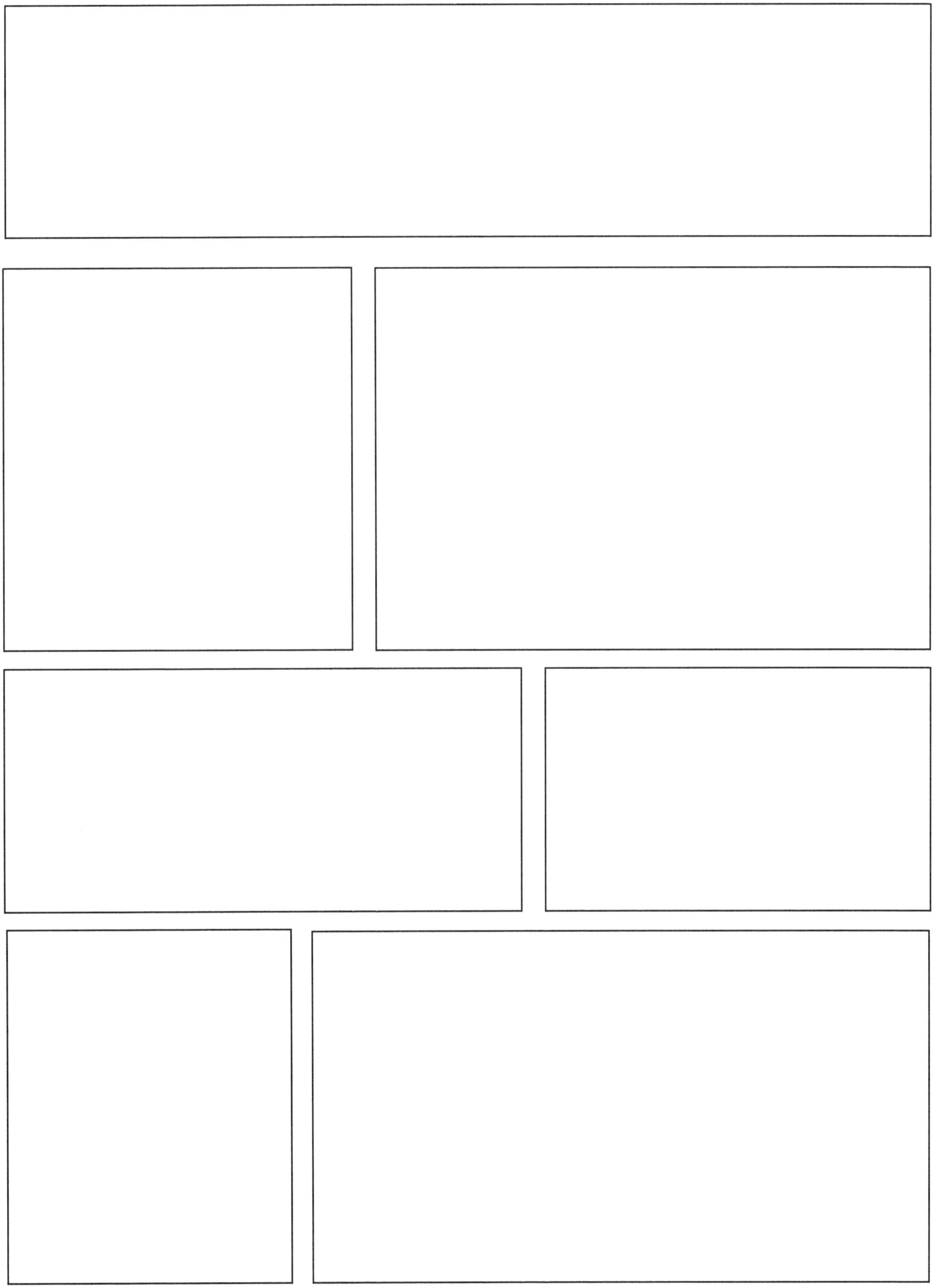

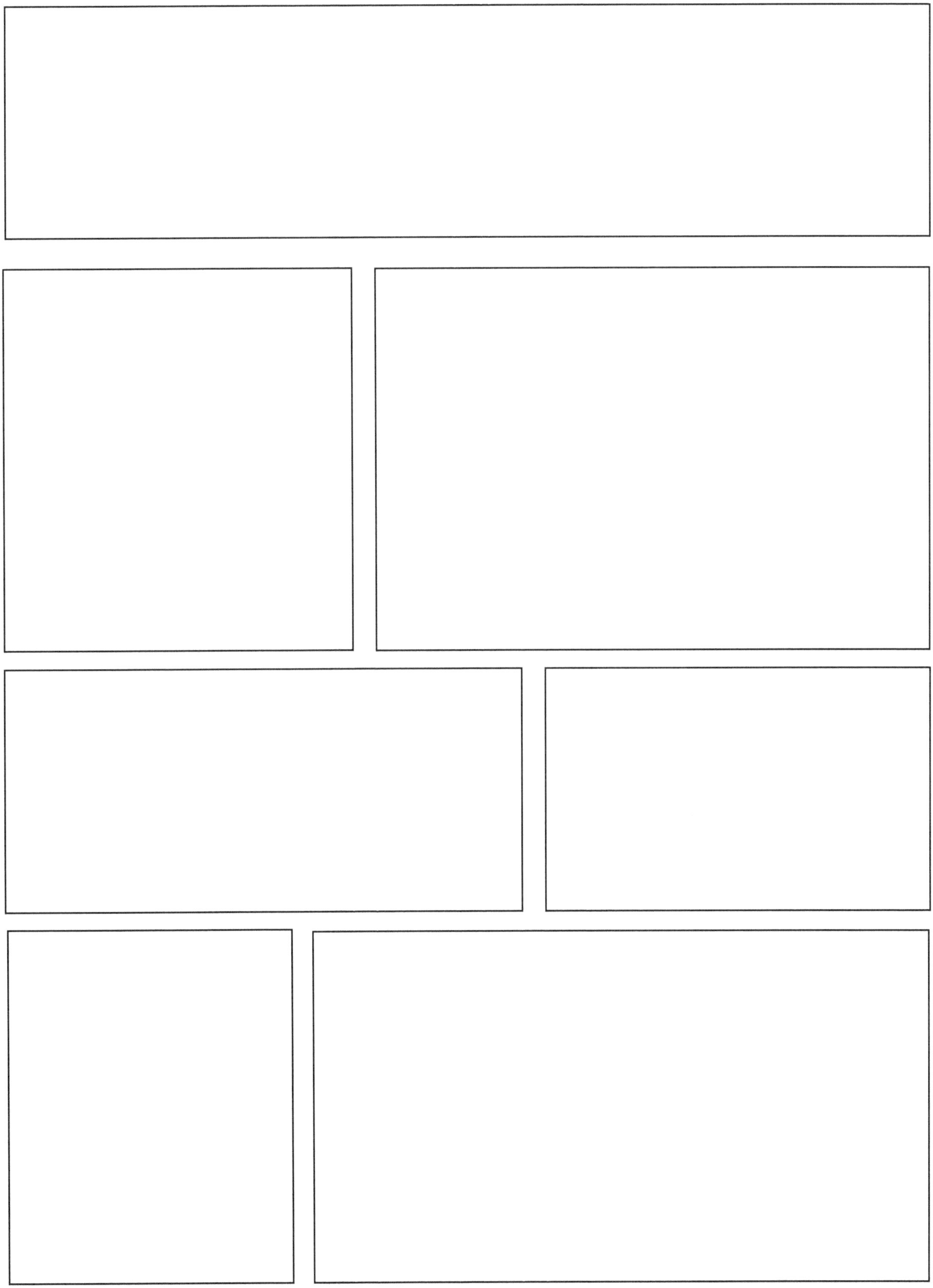

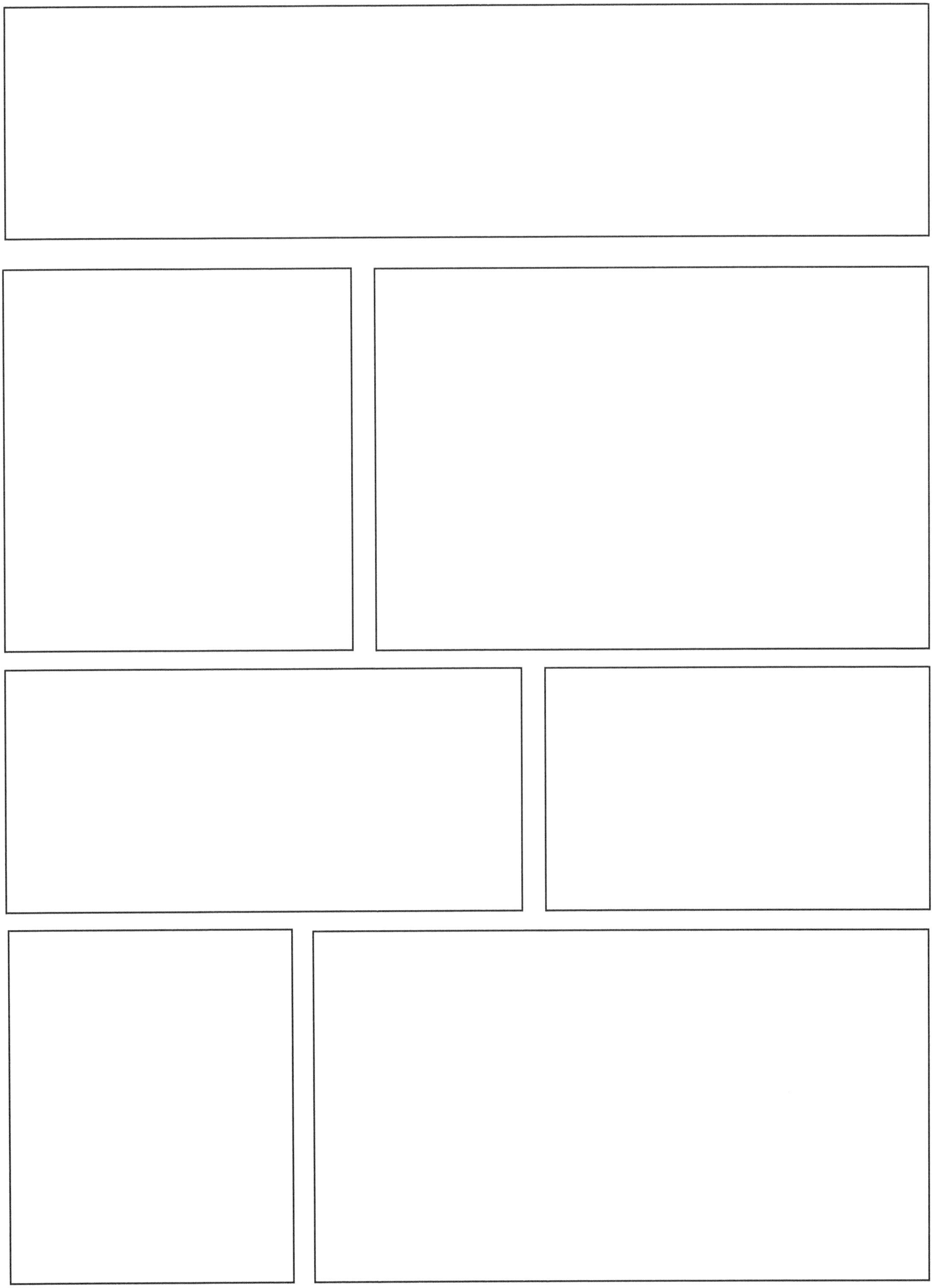

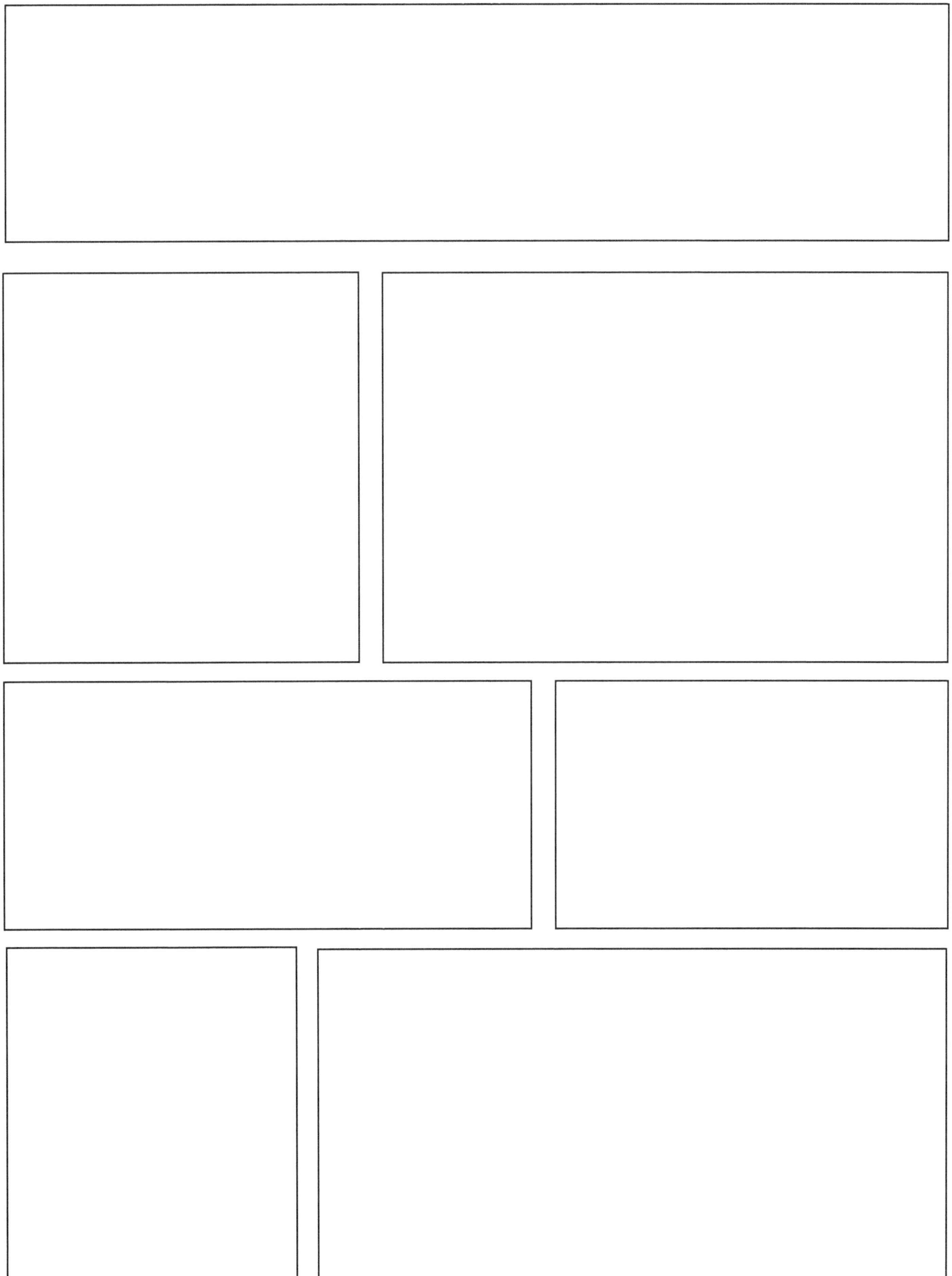

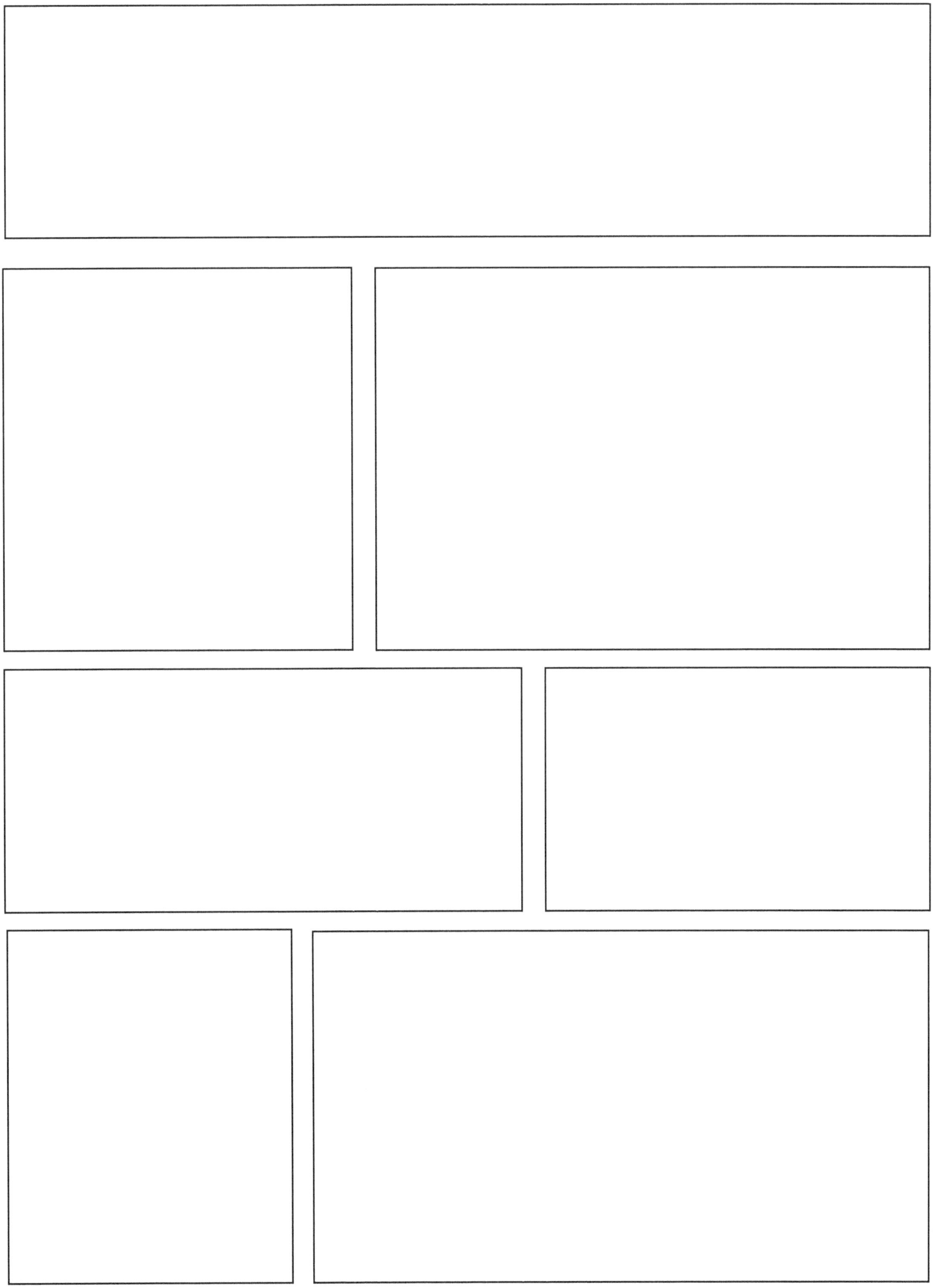

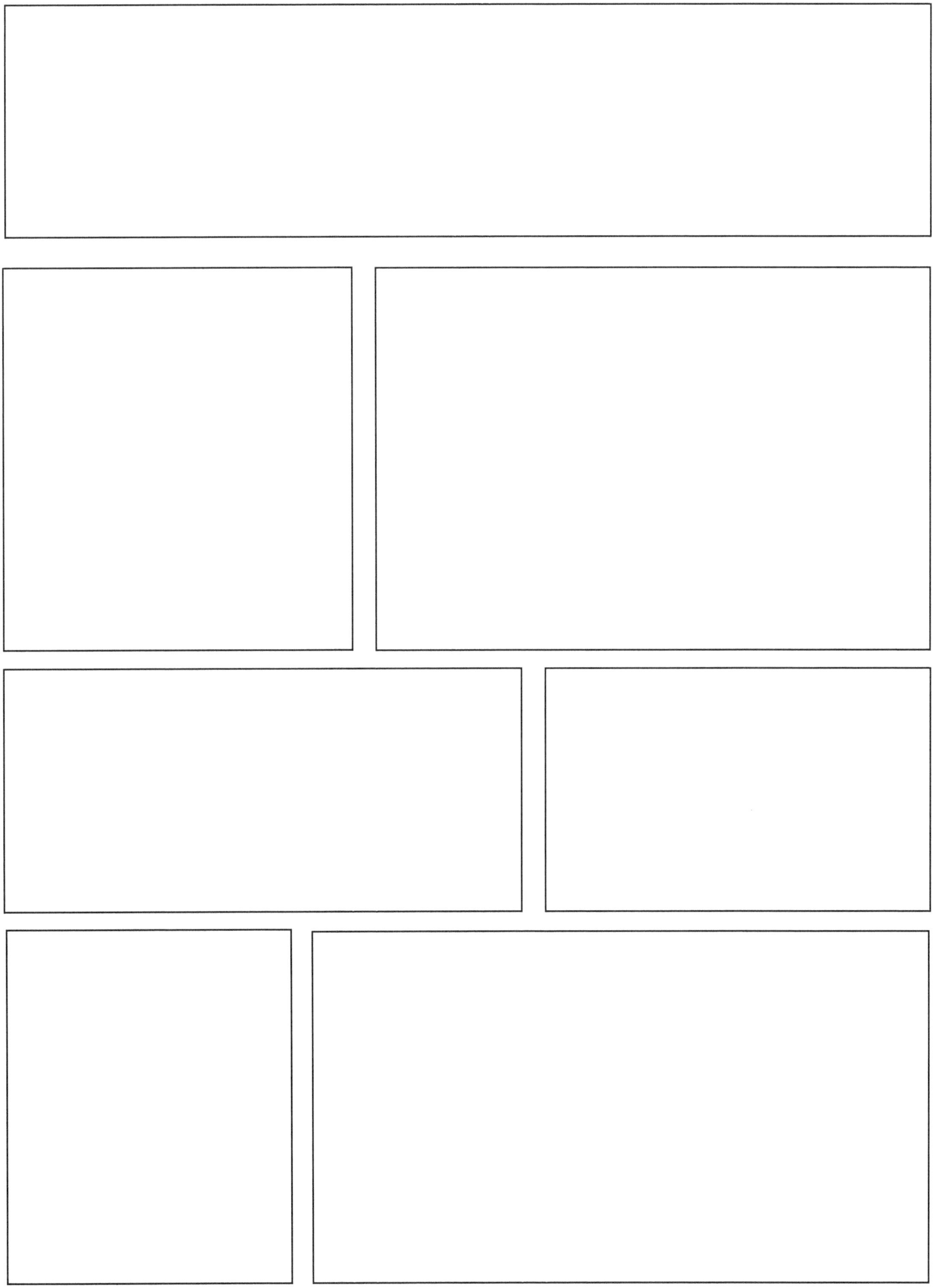

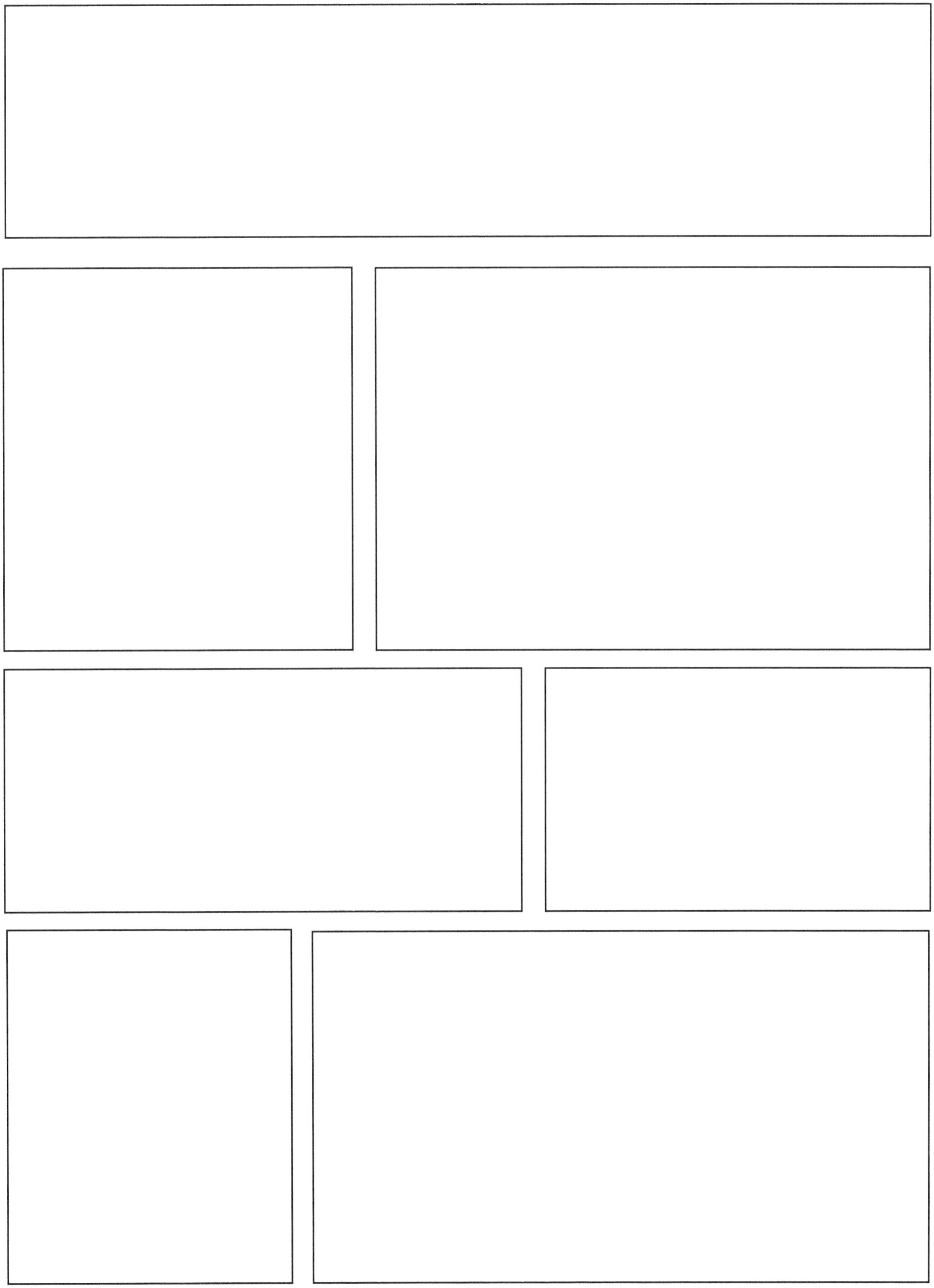

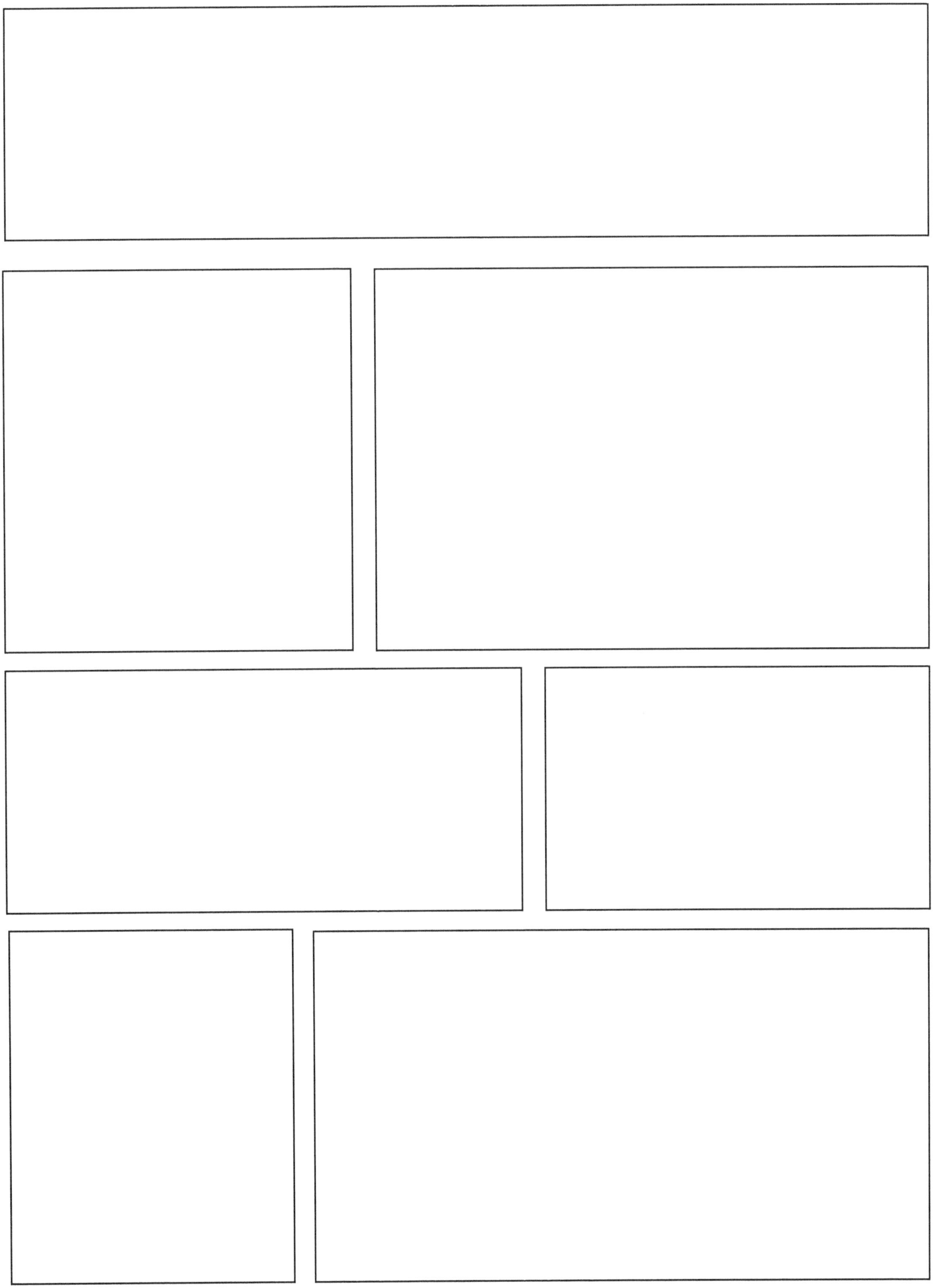

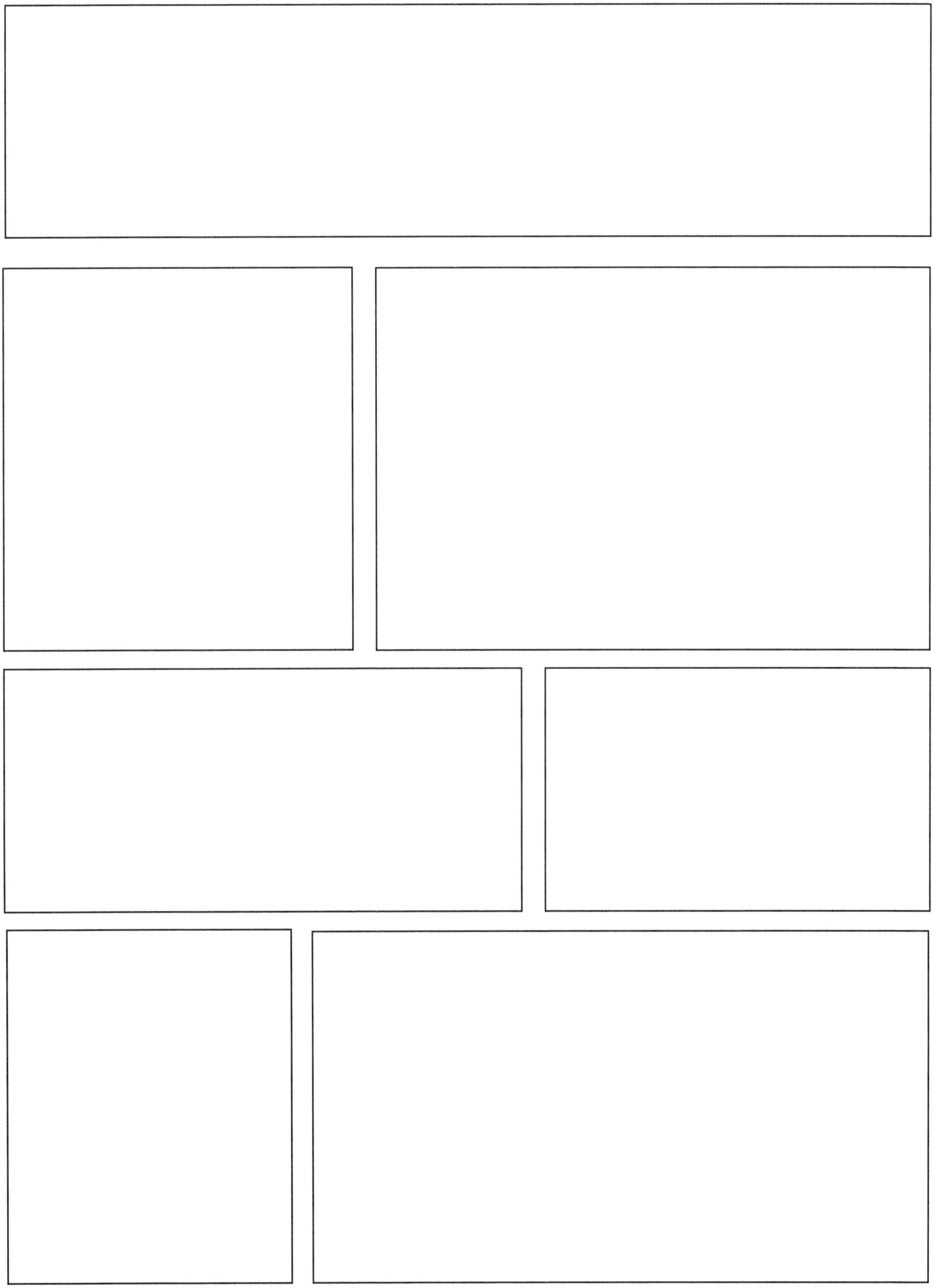

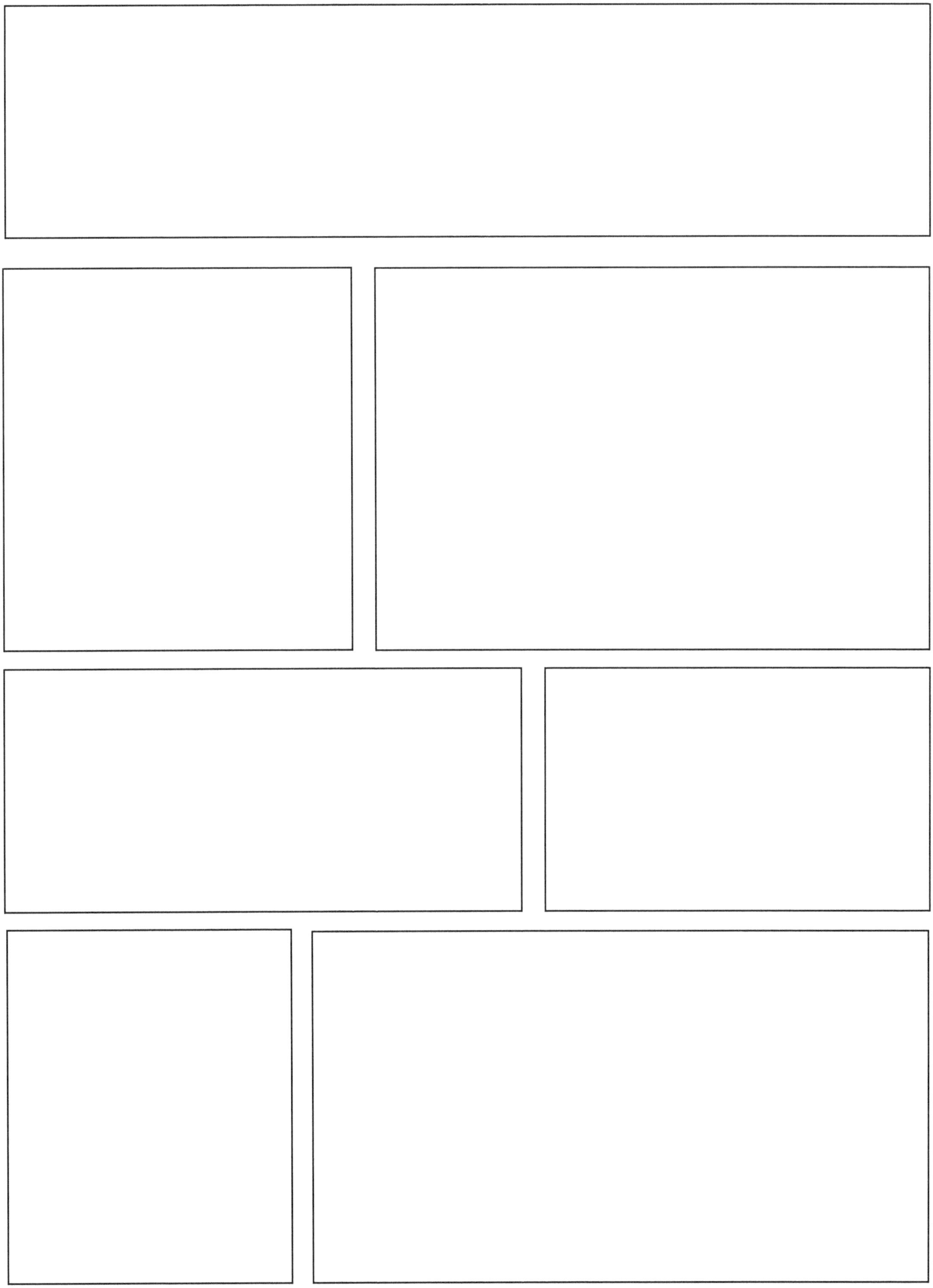

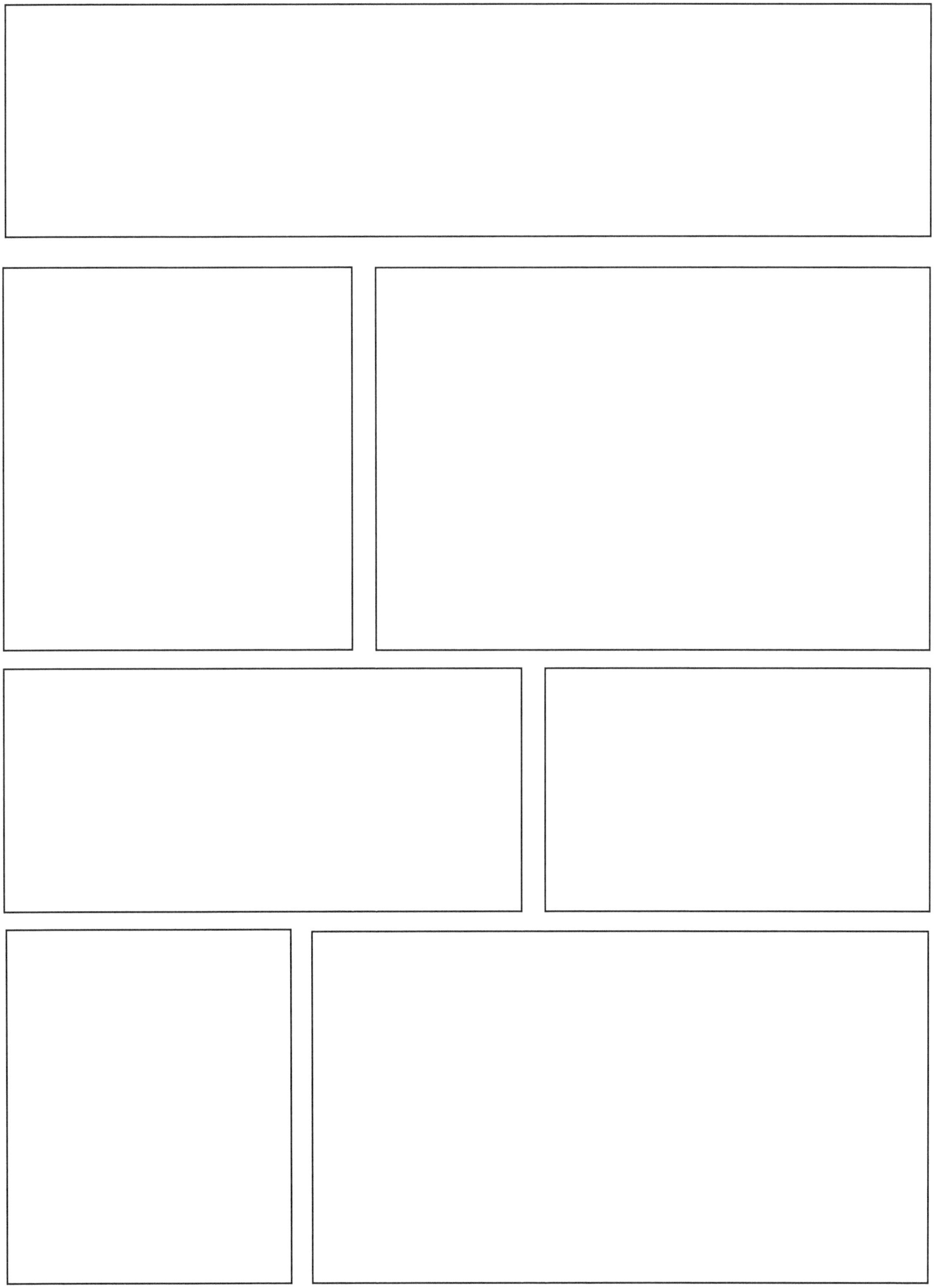

www.ingramcontent.com/pod-product-compliance
Lightning Source LLC
Chambersburg PA
CBHW060420220526
45465CB00008B/2955